the handbook of life
advice on life – reflections from the great and good

Published by Ci Research Ltd., 1st Floor Alderley House, Wilmslow, Cheshire, SK9 1AT. Copyright © Ci Research 2009 All royalties and profits from this book will be donated to Children in Need, Claire House, Francis House and Beechwood Cancer Care. All rights reserved. No part of this publication may be reproduced, stored in a retrieval system, or transmitted in any form or by any means electronic, mechanical, photocopying, recording or otherwise, without the prior permission of Ci Research Ltd.
Printed in Great Britain by Encompass Print Solutions Ltd., Derbyshire.

This book has been compiled and produced by Ci Research Ltd. to commemorate the company's 20th year. The net proceeds - all revenue less production and distribution costs - are to be donated to the following charities:

> Children in Need
> Francis House Children's Hospice
> Claire House Children's Hospice
> Beechwood Cancer Care Centre

Our thanks go to all those who have made this possible: the 'great and good' for their contributions and the 'Book team' at Ci for their time and efforts - in particular Amy, Kez and Sarah. Thanks also to the many others who have freely given their services in favour of the charities supported... Nim in Cambridge, Raph at MGS, Julie in Cornwall, Justine at A4e, Andy at Matrix, Rymans, Theo Paphitis... the list goes on.

As a result of everyone's help, we estimate that approximately 70% of all revenue from the sale of this book will be available for donation.

Our final thanks of course to those supporting these charities by purchasing this book.

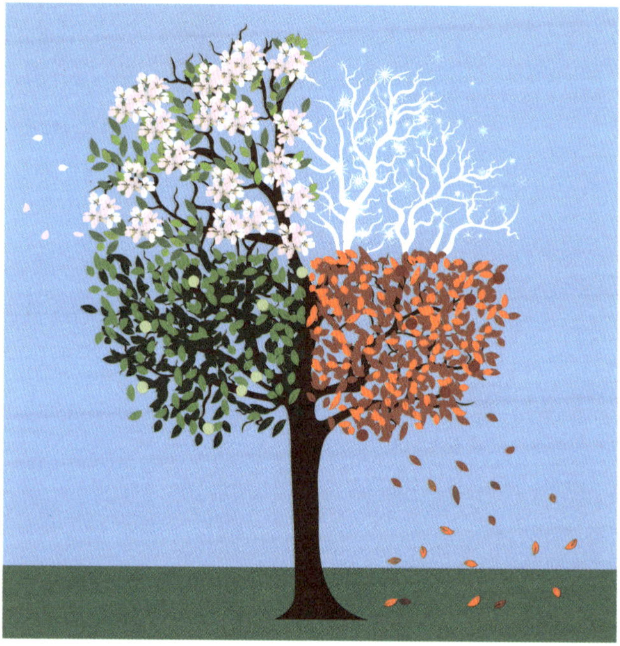

Mel Brooks

The Oscar winning American film director, screenwriter, composer, lyricist, comedian, actor and producer Mel Brooks, is best known for the films Blazing Saddles and The Producers.

> " Look, I don't want to wax philosophic, but I will say that if you're alive you've got to flap your arms and legs, you've got to jump around a lot, for life is the very opposite of death, and therefore you must at very least think noisy and colourfully, or you're not alive. "

Astronomer Royal Lord Martin Rees

Baron Martin Rees of Ludlow is a leading cosmologist and astrophysicist. He is the Astronomer Royal and Master of Trinity College, Cambridge. He has made significant contributions to the field of cosmic microwave background radiation and quasars.

> " One of the wisest remarks I know should serve as a salutary warning to all of us: it's that most people spend most of their lives doing neither what they want to do nor what they ought to be doing. "

Photo by David Levenson/Getty Images

First Lady Michelle Obama

Michelle Obama, mother, lawyer and first African-American First Lady of the United States. Michelle is married to the forty-fourth President of the United States, Barack Obama.

> " One of the lessons that I grew up with was to always stay true to yourself and never let what somebody else says distract you from your goals. And so when I hear about negative and false attacks, I really don't invest any energy in them, because I know who I am. "

Photo by Pascal Le Segretain/Getty Images

Lord Sebastian Coe

Lord Sebastian Coe won two gold and two silver Olympic medals during his career as a middle distance runner, as well as setting twelve world records. A Conservative MP and life peer in 2000, he headed the London bid for the 2012 Olympics and is currently the Chairman of the London Organising Committee for the 2012 Olympic Games.

> "Never be afraid to do it differently."

Ricky Hatton

Down to earth boxer Ricky Hatton enjoyed huge success in the international boxing arena, winning numerous World Titles including the WBA Welterweight Championship. The highlight of Ricky's career was his defeat of the legendary Kostya Tszyu in Manchester. He was awarded an MBE in 2007.

> To me the meaning of life means working hard to provide the best I can for my son Campbell. The best piece of advice I ever received was when I was fighting at the MEN Arena in Manchester. My mum Carol was ringside with my dad and was all excited. She offered the best advice she could when I was being punched by my opponent "Duck Son". Not surprisingly I did and he missed. I love my mum.
> My most life-changing experience?
> I suppose when I beat Kostya Tszyu in front of 22,000 people at the MEN Arena Manchester and became the undisputed champion of the world at light welterweight. I think that moment will stay with me forever. I was accepted and recognised as the best light welterweight in the world and my world changed, it lead to massive fights and more world titles in America.

Paddy Power

Paddy Power is the name behind Ireland's largest bookmaker. The business was founded in 1988 by the merger of three existing Irish main street bookmakers. It is a publicly quoted company, listed on the Irish and UK stock markets. The business has a reputation for funny and often controversial advertising and branding.

> " This one liner from my Dad just before I went to university has always stuck with me. Never be afraid to ask and always be prepared to answer. It's quite a simple motto which is a very helpful sanity check. It reminds me to be confident enough in myself not to pretend I know it all, and to be able to stand over everything I do. "

Uri Geller

Uri Geller, the Israeli English entertainer, is best known for his spoon bending ability and paranormal powers. At the peak of his career in the 1970s, he worked full-time, performing for television audiences worldwide.

" Be positive, optimistic and believe in yourself. "

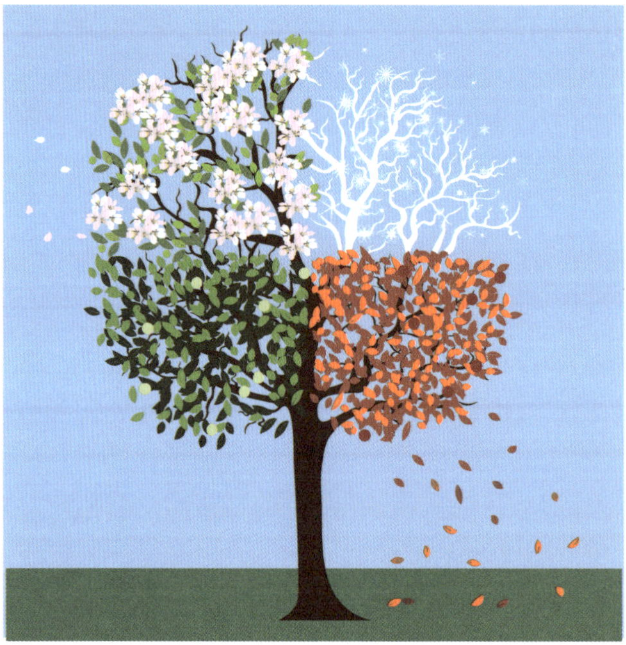

Advice on life from the past

Don't go around saying the world owes you a living. The world owes you nothing. It was here first. ***Mark Twain***

Let your food be your medicine, and your medicine be your food. Walking is man's best medicine. ***Hippocrates***

Give me six hours to chop down a tree and I will spend the first four sharpening the axe - preparation is all.

In the end, it's not the years in your life that count. It's the life in your years. ***Abraham Lincoln***

Some other wise advice.....

There are three types of people in this world: those who make things happen, those who watch things happen and those who wonder "what the hell happened!".

Dalai Lama

Tenzin Gyatso; The Fourteenth Dalai Lama.

" I believe the purpose of life is to be happy. I don't know whether the universe, with its countless galaxies, stars and planets, has a deeper meaning or not but, at the very least, it is clear that we humans who live on this earth face the task of making a happy life for ourselves. Therefore, it is important to discover what will bring about the greatest degree of happiness.

Of the two types of happiness and suffering (i.e. mental and physical), it is the mind that exerts the greatest influence on most of us; and hence we should devote our most serious efforts to bringing about mental peace.

From my own limited experience I have found that the greatest degree of inner tranquillity comes from the development of love and compassion.

The more we care for the happiness of others, the greater our own sense of well-being becomes. This helps remove whatever fears or insecurities we may have and gives us the strength to cope with any obstacles we encounter. It is the ultimate source of success in life.

So, the key to a happier and more successful life and world is the growth of compassion. We do not need to become religious, nor do we need to believe in an ideology. All that is necessary is for each of us to develop our good human qualities. "

This has been extracted from a larger response provided by the Dalai Lama.

Vivienne Westwood DBE

Vivienne Westwood: school teacher come fashion designer who brought Punk into the mainstream. She now has a string of shops and labels under her belt.

" I think it is terribly important to have opinions, and to think. We live in a world of action without thought. "

Steve Smith

Steve Smith is a retired high jumper from England is Britain's most successful high jumper and Olympic Bronze Medallist. He is also a director of Raise the Bar, a training company that uses sport as an inspirational learning model.

> "Through my time in sport, I have come across some great coaches and all of the best ones have exactly the same philosophy – use failure as a motivation. The world's greatest ever sportsman Michael Jordan once said, "I've missed more than 900 shots in my career, I've lost more than 300 games, 26 times I've been trusted to take the game shot and I've missed. I've failed over and over again in my life and that why I succeed". The baggage of past experiences weighs heavily and we stop taking risks, we stay in our comfort zone and we never get to learn from failure. We should be creating a culture of people who are prepared to take a chance and achieve great things. So my best advice came directly from sport and, as Wayne Gretsky (Canadian hockey player) once said, "you miss 100% of the shots that you never take"."

Suzy Aitchison

Suzy Aitchison is a British television actress. Most notable was her recent role in 'Jam & Jerusalem'.

" The meaning of life, well….. Just live it.

As for advice, Don't anticipate disaster. "

Nicholas Clegg MP

Nick Clegg is leader of the Liberal Democrats and British Member of Parliament for Sheffield Hallam. He studied Social Anthropology at Cambridge.

> " Remember that if you want to stand up for the weak, you have to stand up to the powerful. "

Roger Black MBE

Olympic 400m Silver Medalist Roger Black represented Great Britain in World Athletics for 14 years. He won 15 major championship medals and was awarded with an MBE in 1992.

> " If it was easy, then everyone would be doing it. This was said to me by Daley Thompson, the great Decathlete. Early on in my career I was struggling with an injury, really feeling sorry for myself and feeling that it was just too much of a struggle. I couldn't see the light at the end of the tunnel and I remember telling Daley that I didn't know if I could cope. Daley turned to me and said "Roger, if it was easy, then everyone would be doing it." That was true. I guess it's corny, but when the going gets tough, the tough get going. It taught me that if anything is worth achieving, it would always be hard. It was never meant to be easy. "

Sir Terry Wogan

The veteran Radio presenter Sir Terry Wogan has worked for the BBC for most of his career. He is best known for his BBC Radio 2 programme, Children in Need and Eurovision Song Contest commentary.

> " Life has no meaning if all you think of is yourself.
>
> The best advice on life would be... God never closes one door, but shuts another (twist on an old Irish proverb) – so, open your own doors... "

Paul McGee

Paul McGee is an international speaker and author. Over the last five years he has been developing the S.U.M.O. Principles as a way of helping people achieve better results in life.

> " The meaning of life for me is: To find out your purpose for being on this Earth, to discover your God given talent and then use it to benefit others. The best piece of advice is: Remember the formula E + R = O. It's not the Event, but how you Respond that determines the Outcome. My life changing experience was winning a public speaking competition at school and realising that I might be the last person to be picked for the football team. I might struggle with maths and I have the manual dexterity of a penguin, but at least I can use my words to good effect! "

A few facts on life.

If you are right handed, you will tend to chew your food on your right side. If you are left handed, you will tend to chew your food on your left side.

When you blush, the lining of your stomach also turns red.

We all share our birthday with at least 9 million other people in the world.... Wow - what a party you could have.

The only part of the body that has no blood supply is the cornea in the eye. It takes in oxygen directly from the air.

Human hair normally grows at the rate of 15.24cm per year.

Earth is almost five billion years old, although life has only existed on the planet for the last 150 to 200 million years. This means that life has been present on the planet for only 5%-10% of its lifetime.

The body has two million sweat glands.

Once a human reaches the age of 35, he/she will start losing approximately 7,000 brain cells a day. The cells will never be replaced.

Did you know that there are 206 bones in the adult human body and there are 300 in children (as they grow some of the bones fuse together).

The ears of a cricket are located on the front legs, just below the knee.

The average human body contains enough: Sulphur to kill all fleas on an average dog, carbon to make 900 pencils, potassium to fire a toy cannon, fat to make 7 bars of soap, phosphorus to make 2,200 match heads, and enough water to fill a ten-gallon tank.

Up to the age of six or seven months a child can breathe and swallow at the same time. An adult cannot do this.

A few facts on life.

Six-year-olds laugh an average of 300 times a day. Adults only laugh around 60 times a day.

Every person has a unique tongue print.

All of the DNA in an adult human body could fit inside one ice cube, but if unwound, stretched out and joined end to end, it would reach from the earth to the sun and back again more than 400 times.

A Swiss study found that a majority of women unconsciously choose mates with a body odour that differs from their own natural scents, which, as a result, ensures better immune protection for their children.

Sweden has the lowest birth rate in the world.

Earth is gradually slowing down. Every few years, an extra second is added to make up for lost time. Millions of years ago, a day on Earth will have been 20 hours long. It is believed that, after a few million years, a day on Earth will be 27 hours long.

Despite being called Earth, only 29% of the surface is actually 'earth' (land). The rest of the planet's surface (71%) is made up of water.

Just about 3 people are born every second somewhere in the world and about 1.3333 people die every second.

In 30 minutes, the average body gives off enough heat (combined) to bring a half gallon of water to boil.

The average UK male spends 8.8 years of their life being ill, with the average UK female being ill for 10.6 years (Office for National Statistics' Social Trends survey, 2007).

In one day your heart beats 100,000 times.

Men are officially the best at changing a baby. Research shows that the average time taken by a woman to change a baby is 2 minutes and 5 seconds - but the average man takes only 1 minute and 36 seconds.

Tom Hingley

Tom Hingley is best known as lead singer of 90's rock band Inspiral Carpets. He has gone on to have a successful solo career and now fronts new band The Lovers.

" The best bit of advice I have ever been given was given to me by DJ and legend John Peel. He said that you should never lie to people, not because it is morally incorrect but also because you always have to remember what you have said to people the next time you see them. Great advice from a wonderful and sadly missed person. "

Richard Dawkins

Richard Dawkins is a British biological theorist, evolutionary biologist, author and outspoken atheist. He popularised the gene-centred view of evolution, and introduced the meme concept.

> " My father once told me, "it is never too late to start". "

Photo by Luciana Whitaker/LatinContent/Getty Images

Willy Russell

Willy is a British dramatist, lyricist, and composer. Best-known for his works Educating Rita, Shirley Valentine, and Blood Brothers. He received BAFTA and Oscar nominations for Best Adapted Screenplay for both Educating Rita and Shirley Valentine.

" Whenever I'm asked to give advice, I usually respond by saying "Always beware of those who would give you advice".

I do, though, allow one exception and enthusiastically pass on this particular gem of advice to what is, I hope, only a tiny handful of those who would need it - "Should you ever find yourself in that wretched situation where, having imbibed a little too fully, you can now no longer lie down or close your eyes without the room going into a nausea-inducing spin, the only solution is to lie flat on your left side and rest your head on your outstretched left arm". There's probably some sound scientific reason for the effectiveness of this procedure but I've never discovered what it is. I just know from experience that it really does work. "

Paula Rego

Paula Rego is a Portuguese painter, illustrator and printmaker. She was born in Lisbon, although her family later moved to Britain. Paula was educated in English schools and attended the Slade School of Art.

> " The best advice on life I have ever been given was from a dear friend, a long time ago, who said "Stop farting around, and get on with your work". "

Nelson Mandela

Nelson Mandela is one of the world's most revered statesmen. He spent 27 years in prison for political crimes before being elected South Africa's first black president in 1994.

> " I learned that courage was not the absence of fear, but the triumph over it. I felt fear myself more time than I can remember, but I hid it behind a mask of boldness. The brave man is not he who does not feel afraid, but he who conquers fear. "

Mayer Hersh

Mayer is a Manchester-based survivor of the Holocaust. Having emerged from hell almost unscathed, Mayer attributes his survival in part to his ability to cling to hope when everyone around him lost theirs.

> " His ideal is to live in freedom, devoid of fear, surrounded by many good friends, and to bring happiness and contentment for himself and others. "

Rafael Benitez

Rafael Benitez is best known for being the current manager of Liverpool Football Club, having led them to victory in both the UEFA Champions League and the F.A. Cup. His career began at the Real Madrid academy and included successful spells managing Tenerife and Valencia football clubs.

> " I have received a lot of advice every year since I was a young man. It was my father who gave me this advice; Maybe the best is to think before you speak. "

Theo Paphitis

Theo Paphitis was once an assistant tea boy working at a Lloyds of London broker. He now stars in BBC TV's Dragons' Den, is Chairman of the stationery specialists Ryman and with fellow dragon Peter Jones, owns the experience company, Red Letter Days. He is best known for revitalising businesses, such as Stationery Box, Parners, La Senza and Contessa plus his success as Chairman of Millwall Football Club.

> " Life is not a dress rehearsal. You need to make the most of every minute of your waking day and live as though it's your last, with no regrets and a clear conscience. Live 'in the moment' and focus on the here and now. As they say: yesterday is history, tomorrow is a mystery but today is a gift. That's why it is called the present. "

Photo by Dave Hogan/Getty Images

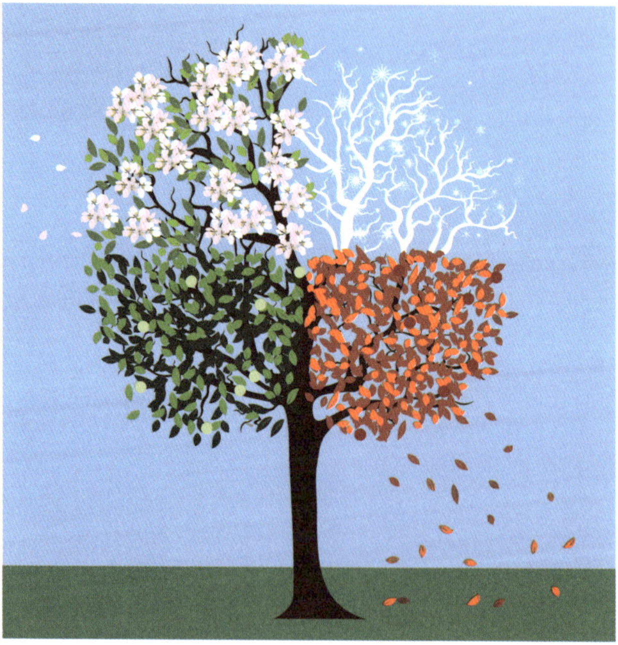

More advice on life from the past

Success is not final, failure is not fatal: it is the courage to continue that counts.
A pessimist sees the difficulty in every opportunity; an optimist sees the opportunity in every difficulty.
Winston Churchill

Adversity has ever been considered the state in which a man most easily becomes acquainted with himself.
What is easy is seldom excellent. *Samuel Johnson*

Do not dwell in the past, do not dream of the future, concentrate the mind on the present moment. *Buddha*

Some other wise advice.....

The person who says it cannot be done should not interrupt the person doing it.

Dr. Sree Sreedharan

Sreedharan is a disciple of the internationally eminent philosopher, Swami Parthasarathy. Having completed the three year residential course at the Vedanta Academy, Sreedharan has dedicated his life to study, research and to propagate Vedanta philosophy and its practical application to life.

> "Parents should command respect and not demand respect. If they demand respect, they will never get it. Parents can command respect only when they set an example for their kids. I would also add that life is not measured by the number of breaths we take, but by the moments that take our breath away."

Swami Parthasarathy

Swami Parthasarathy's writings, discourses and seminars have met with outstanding response all over the world for over fifty years. He has been covered in print and television media worldwide and is known for his personal counselling to business, sport and film celebrities.

> " Thinking is an art, a skill, a technique. You must learn and practice it as you would the violin, golf or bridge. Intelligence is acquired from schools and universities while the intellect is developed by oneself. Humans need an intellect to resolve the dilemma of choice and act. "

The Duke of Westminster

The title Duke of Westminster was created by Queen Victoria in 1874, The current Duke is Gerald Grosvenor, 6th Duke of Westminster.

> " The best piece of advice given to me is the poem "If" by Rudyard Kipling. "

Rudyard Kipling was born in Bombay on December 30th 1865. He spent his first five years of life in Bombay, but was then sent back to England to stay with a foster family. At the age of 12 he went to college in the United States. When he was 16 he returned to Lahore to live with his parents and started working on a local magazine. It was here that he started to write poetry and stories. During his life he declined many of the honours which had been offered him, including a knighthood, the Poet Laureateship, and the Order of Merit, but in 1907 he had accepted the Nobel Prize for Literature. The poem 'If' is one of his most famous, and is said to be based on the personal qualities of his friend and acquaintance Dr. Leander Starr Jameson, a colonial statesman – which Kipling saw as an inspiration for the characteristics he recommended young people to live by. Kipling wrote 'If' in the year 1896, when aged 31.

Photo by Gemma Levine/Getty Images

If

If you can keep your head when all about you
Are losing theirs and blaming it on you,
If you can trust yourself when all men doubt you,
But make allowance for their doubting too;
If you can wait and not be tired by waiting,
Or being lied about, don't deal in lies,
Or being hated, don't give way to hating,
And yet don't look too good, nor talk too wise:
If you can dream - and not make dreams your master,
If you can think - and not make thoughts your aim;
If you can meet with Triumph and Disaster
And treat those two impostors just the same;
If you can bear to hear the truth you've spoken
Twisted by knaves to make a trap for fools,
Or watch the things you gave your life to, broken,
And stoop and build 'em up with worn-out tools:
If you can make one heap of all your winnings
And risk it all on one turn of pitch-and-toss,
And lose, and start again at your beginnings
And never breath a word about your loss;
If you can force your heart and nerve and sinew
To serve your turn long after they are gone,
And so hold on when there is nothing in you
Except the Will which says to them: "Hold on!"
If you can talk with crowds and keep your virtue,
Or walk with kings - nor lose the common touch,
If neither foes nor loving friends can hurt you,
If all men count with you, but none too much;
If you can fill the unforgiving minute
With sixty seconds' worth of distance run,
Yours is the Earth and everything that's in it,
And - which is more - you'll be a Man, my son!

Mike Atherton

Mike Atherton, right handed England cricket captain turned journalist and commentator. He captained England in a record 49 test matches and is now cricket correspondent for The Times.

> When I was starting out on a life in sport my father said to me not to worry about off-field issues, such as money, because if you look after the cricket itself then everything else would fall into place. Later, my agent, a chap called Jon Holmes, said to me - and this could be considered to be worrying for an agent - never do anything for money. What they were both trying to say in their own way was that it was important to find out what interests you, what gives you a buzz, and follow your passion and everything else will come from that. Finding out what interests you is the hardest but ultimately most rewarding thing in life.

Boris Johnson

Current Mayor of London, Boris Johnson, previously served as the Conservative Member of Parliament for Henley-on-Thames and as editor of The Spectator magazine.

> " Best bit of advice was from my grandmother when she said to me "Darling, it's not how you're doing; it's what you're doing." "

Archbishop of Westminster Vincent Nichols

Vincent Nichols is President of the Catholic Bishops' conference of England and Wales, and spokesman for the Roman Catholic Church in England and Wales.

> Always try to see what is good in any person you meet. Sometimes that is not easy to do. Only when you see and recognise what is good in others can you start to build relationships with them.

John Thomson

John Thomson is a comedian and actor, known for his roles in The Fast Show and Cold Feet. His most recent roles include Coronation Street and narrating Ghosthunting With... on ITV2.

> " The greatest successes are always learned from failure. The ability to get back on the horse once you've fallen off shows true spirit. "

Best bit of advice straight from the Charities.....

Beechwood Cancer Care Centre

The best bit of advice on life given to me is: 'On each day do the best you can with what you've got, where you're at'. For me as a cancer patient, but also somebody who has been in recovery from addiction for seven years now, this is how I try to live my life on a daily basis. Also, life is precious, so live in the now. Be grateful every day and accept life on life's terms.
Bernadette Tansey - Cancer Patient

To love and to be loved.
Michelle Nixon - Nurse Councillor

Claire House Hospice

Happiness keeps you sweet, Trials keep you strong, Sorrows keep you human, Failures keep you humble, Success keeps you glowing, But only you keeps you going.
Barbara Maddock - Appeals Team

Don't worry, about a thing, coz every little thing, is gonna be alright.
Kirsty Wright - Fundraiser

Make everyday as if it's the last.

Hey, be positive, I spent the day above ground.
Jill Maynard - Appeals Team

Always remember the people you meet on the way up as you are sure to meet them on the way down.
Chris Meaden - Appeals Team

"Only a life lived for others is a life worthwhile" and "Life is just a chance to grow a soul".
Anna Maria Picariello - Appeals Team

"To love and be loved"
Laura Breen, Fundraiser

Maurizio Fondriest

Maurizio Fondriest is a retired Italian professional road racing cyclist. He won the world championship in 1988. Since retiring, he set up his own bicycle manufacturer called Fondriest, which makes carbon fibre bicycles.

" Some years ago, the two year old child of a dear friend was diagnosed with cancer of the kidneys and I shared with him moments of fear for his child. Fortunately, the outcome was good. The experience helped me appreciate life so much and made me realise how fortunate I was not to have experienced this with my own children. Afterwards, my friend and I created a charity to help children who were ill or had other difficulties.
I feel privileged that, through the success and fame I have achieved in my sporting career, I have been able to help people less fortunate than me.
So my advice would be to appreciate so much the health of your children and not to take this for granted; and wherever you can, help others who are less fortunate. "

Margaret Thatcher

Margaret Thatcher served as leader of the Conservative Party from 1975 to 1990 and was Prime Minister of the United Kingdom from 1979 to 1990. To date she is the only woman to have held either post, and was awarded a life peerage in 1992.

" Disciplining yourself to do what you know is right and important, although difficult, is the highroad to pride, self-esteem, and personal satisfaction. "

Professor Geoffrey Beattie

Professor Geoffrey Beattie is Head of School and Dean of Psychological Sciences at the University of Manchester. A well known TV presenter, journalist and author, he has also been awarded the Spearman Medal.

> The best bit of advice on life I ever got was from my mother who used to say to me 'Remember you've only got one mother, you can have many women in your life but only one mother.' I was about twenty one, she was widowed and living alone. I took it, at the time, as this desperate plea to treat her better, to give her more attention. I thought that the 'advice' was selfishly motivated and therefore I didn't value it. But I can now see the merit in what she was saying. I came from a working class background with everything to work for. I put my career first and my family, unfortunately, second. I suspect that this will be a source of endless regret. In the end it is the closest ties, the biological ties, which are the most important. It took me many years to realise this, but if I had just listened to this piece of advice more carefully in the first place, I might have understood sooner.

George Osborne MP

Conservative Party politician George Osborne has been the Member of Parliament for Tatton since 2001. He is currently Shadow Chancellor of the Exchequer.

> " The best bit of advice I have ever received was: Stay true to your principles. "

Lewis Hamilton

Racing driver Lewis Hamilton is the youngest ever Formula One World Champion. He currently races for McLaren Mercedes and was awarded an MBE in March 2009.

> " I'm given advice all the time; from my engineers instructing me to push when I'm out on the track, to my supporters telling me to go out and win the race for them. But the best advice on my own life always comes from my family. And it's been simple: never lose sight of who you are and where you've come from; love and respect your family and never lose sight of your dreams, no matter how hard they become. To that, I can also add: 'never give up;' even when everybody else thinks you're finished, I've kept pushing, and that can get you to some incredible places. "

Col. Tim Collins OBE

Tim Collins OBE, former colonel in the British Army. He's best known for his role in the Iraq War in 2003, and his inspirational eve-of-battle speech.

> " In life, listen carefully, contemplate and where you can, add value. If you cannot add value then learn from the experience; avoid doing things for the sake of it and so do no harm. "

Photo by Ian Waldie/Getty Images

Sir Ian Botham

Former England Test Cricketer and team Captain, Ian Botham is a genuine all rounder. He currently commentates for Sky Sports and has been a prominent fundraiser for charity.

> " When I am asked about such matters my response is: "Ride the torpedo to the end of the tube", in other words anything you undertake in life give 100+%. "

Frank Field MP

Labour Politician Frank Field has been a Member of Parliament for Birkenhead since 1979. He believes strongly in fighting climate change, and co-founded the charity Cool Earth.

> " The day my mother died she commented that she had never knowingly done harm to anyone. She was too modest to say that she spent most of her life doing good. That is not a bad ideal. "

Benjamin Franklin

This is an often quoted phrase from Benjamin Franklin, who back in the 18th century, came up with a good few bits of advice on life himself....

Up, sluggard, and waste not life; in the grave will be sleeping enough.

Well done is better than well said.

A good example is the best sermon.

He that is good for making excuses is seldom good for anything else.

More advice on life from the past

He has achieved success who has lived well,

laughed often and loved much;

Who has gained the respect of intelligent men and

the love of little children;

Who has filled his niche and accomplished his task;

Who has left the world better than he found it;

Who has looked for the best in others

and given the best he had;

Whose life was an inspiration;

Whose memory is a benediction.

Robert Louis Stevenson

In memory of Alan Rousseau

Sir Alex Ferguson

Sir Alex Ferguson is best known for managing Manchester United. He started his career as a player for Queens Park and had a spell managing Scotland. He received a knighthood for services to football in 1999.

" When I was 21 I was out of football for 6/7 weeks with a broken eyebrow and cheek. I had previously been playing reserve football and was contemplating going to Canada to live, but when I came back I scored a hatrick against Rangers at Ibrox playing for St Johnstone's first team. I was the first player to do this and that's when I thought about a career in football. I have had a few good pieces of advice about life: Appreciate your youth, upbringing and the ideals that your parents have given you and through that you can enjoy life and pass these values to your own children.
You should enjoy it and try and have a happy approach to it.

My Dad told me when I was about to start work: "If you are going to do something, do it well," and I believe that has been much the story of my life. "

Martha Lane Fox

Martha Lane Fox was an icon of the early 00's dotcom boom. She is co-founder of Lastminute.com and has gone on to become a non-executive director of Marks & Spencer, Channel 4 Television and Mydeco.

> " Always be optimistic; try to imagine the best will happen and not the worst. Assume that people will be good not bad and that you can make a difference in whatever you choose to do. "

Photo by Nick Harvey/WireImage

Squadron Leader Graham Duff

Red 8, or Duffy as he is known in the team, is in his second year flying with The Red Arrows. He joined the Royal Air Force in 1996 after gaining a degree in Aeronautical Engineering from Bristol University. He started his operational career flying the ground-attack Jaguar GR3A aircraft and gained extensive experience defending the No Fly Zone in Northern Iraq.

> Never give up. If you want to accomplish something, only you know how you can do it. Negative advice should not be adhered. If you think you can do it, then 99% of the time you can. Ignore the 1% chance that someone else might see and go ahead, achieve your goals.

Senior Aircraftsman Scott Connelly

Scott joined the Royal Air Force in 1997 serving at RAF Lossiemouth, RAF Kinloss and Germany. He has been an Avionics Engineer for The Red Arrows for the past four years. This year he received the accolade of Blue of the Year.

" The best piece of advice I have been given in life, is that if at first you do not succeed try, try again. There may be many obstacles along your fruitful journey to success but do not lose your faith or your focus and keep chasing that dream goal whatever it takes. "

Dharmachari Nagaraja

Dharmachari Nagaraja is a member of the Glasgow Buddhist Centre and often contributes to Terry Wogan's BBC Radio Two programme 'Pause for thought'. He is author of the book 'Buddha at Bedtime'.

> "'Experiences are preceded by mind, led by mind, and produced by mind. If one speaks or acts with an impure mind, suffering follows even as the cartwheel follows the hoof of the ox (drawing the cart)."

From the Dhammapada.

Buddha

Dharmachari Nagaraja provided us with this short Buddha story, which illustrates the choice that we humans have faced in relationship to each other and to life since we first ever learned to get about on two feet.

One day a Buddha visited heaven and then hell. In both realms he saw many people seated at long tables on which were laid out many delicious foods hot and cold, sweet and savoury.

In both heaven and hell, the people sitting at the tables had chopsticks over a metre long tied to their right arms while their left hands and arms were tied to their chairs.

In the hell realm, no matter how much the diners stretched and tried to manoeuvre their arms, the chopsticks were just too long for them to pick up the delicious food and get into their mouths. Growing more and more impatient and hungry, their hands and chopsticks tangled with one another and very quickly the food was scattered and wasted on the floor and they howled in frustration.

However, in heaven realm, the people happily used the long chopsticks to pick out a fellow diners favourite food and to feed it to him, and in turn they were fed by others. They all enjoyed their meal working in harmony.

Every moment we have the opportunity to work together and create heaven or, if we chose, we can create hell.

David Lloyd

English cricketer David Lloyd played county cricket for Lancashire and Test and One Day International cricket for England. He is also a cricket commentator for Sky Sports and is an author, journalist and columnist.

> " Meaning of life? If only I knew. The best advice on life is to be yourself. "

Aliza Olmert

Aliza Olmert is an Israeli artist, photographer, author and social worker. She is married to former Israeli Prime Minister Ehud Olmert.

> " I choose a piece of advice I was given few years ago, while dreaming about establishing "New Beginnings" (a movement to raise consciousness and establish early childhood intervention centres for children from birth to six): If you wish to walk on water, first find out where the rocks on the sea bed lie. "

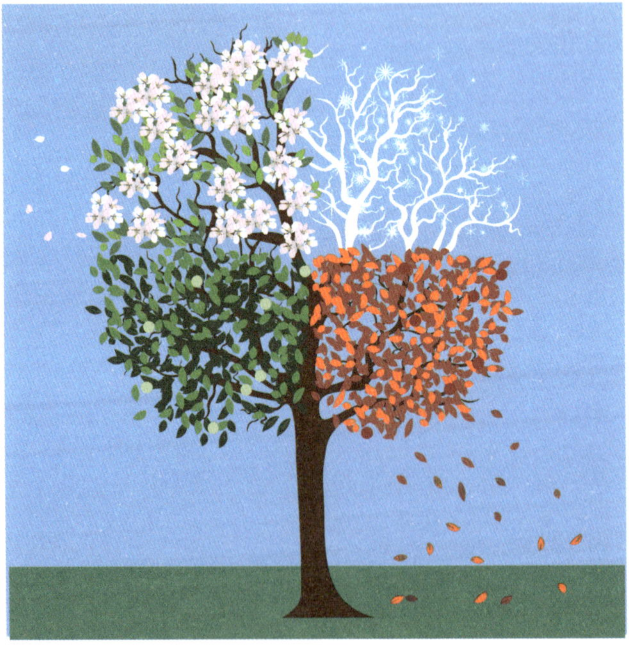

More advice on life from the past

By three methods we may learn wisdom: First, by reflection, which is noblest; Second, by imitation, which is easiest; and third by experience, which is the bitterest. ***Confucius***

A man who dares to waste one hour of time has not discovered the value of life. ***Charles Darwin***

I have a simple philosophy: Fill what's empty. Empty what's full. Scratch where it itches. ***Alice Roosevelt Longworth***

Some other wise advice.....

Some men have a thousand experiences and some have one experience a thousand times - there is a big difference.

Christine Hamilton

Christine Hamilton, a well known British personality, has had a string of successful presenting appearances and is now a renowned conference and after dinner speaker.

" My Mum used to quote those two redoubtable characters from 'The Water Babies' by Charles Kingsley: Mrs. DoAsYouWouldBeDoneBy and Mrs. BeDoneByAsYouDid. Stick to those two and you won't go far wrong! "

David Blunkett MP

David Blunkett is a British Labour politician and a Member of Parliament for Sheffield Brightside since 1987. He became Education Secretary and then Home Secretary in Tony Blair's first Cabinet.

> " The best advice that I have been given and that I always give to young people setting out on life, particularly those facing adversity is: "Never take no for an answer if you know in your heart that you can do it". But also remember that all of us at some point in our lives need support, and one day we might be able to give back a little of what we've gained from the thoughtfulness of others and encourage a sense of mutuality in our highly interdependent world. "

Annie Vernon

Cornish lass Annie Vernon is the Olympic Games silver Quad Scull medal winner and reigning Quad Scull world champion. Annie started rowing at Castle Dore Rowing Club at Golant in Cornwall and continued while at Downing College, Cambridge.

" Meaning of life? It differs for each person depending on their priorities so the important thing is knowing what your priorities are. So, I would turn it on its head: it shouldn't be, what is the meaning of life; but instead, what gives your life meaning? What are the things that are important to you? Once you've discovered that, the rest of life just slots into place.

…and in terms of advice….. there's no such thing as perfection. There's no such thing as a perfect race, or perfect preparation, or the perfect athlete. All you can do is make the best of what you've got and stop always striving for something else. Be the best you can be within yourself, instead of trying to always hunt after something else. This may sound defeatist, but the point is at some point you have to have faith in yourself and your own abilities, and not always think you're never going to be perfect. There's no such thing! "

Chief Rabbi Lord Sacks

Lord Jonathan Sacks is Chief Rabbi of the United Hebrew Congregations of the Commonwealth. Rabbi Sacks was Principal of Jews' College, and Rabbi of the Golders Green and Marble Arch synagogues. He was elevated to the Peerage in October 2009.

> If we are to cherish freedom, and to guard it, we must remember what the alternative is: the bread of affliction and the bitter herbs of slavery.

Debbie Wiseman

Debbie Wiseman studied piano and composition at the Guildhall School of Music and Drama. She has composed for TV and film, and in 2004 she was awarded an MBE in the New Years Honours List for services to the film industry.

" My wonderful composition teacher, Buxton Orr, told me to compose something every day; even if it's rubbish and you throw it out afterwards. It will keep your compositional juices flowing and you'll never be short of ideas. I've found that to be such insightful and clever advice. Composing music for film and television often demands that I write music very fast, and to tight deadlines, so it's important never to run out of ideas or inspiration. By writing every day, the sometimes impossible deadlines imposed by writing for the media never trouble me! "

Lord Patten of Barens CH

Lord Chris Patten was former Member of Parliament, eventually rising to a Cabinet Minister and Party Chairman and in January 2005 he took his seat in the House of Lords.

" Undoubtedly the best piece of advice that I have ever been given was from the lips of my late father; he used to say that since we did not believe in reincarnation in my family we should recognise that we were only on earth once and should make the most of it while we were here! For him being bored, doing nothing or kicking one's heels were capital offences. "

Liz McClarnon

As well as being one third of the girl group Atomic Kitten, Liz McClarnon was also crowned 2008 Master Chef Champion and now makes regular TV appearances as a presenter.

> My life only has meaning with happiness in it, everyday I strive to be happy just for that day and the next day I have the same goal because what have I got to lose? Make life about the good stuff!! I'm grateful for the good stuff and the bad stuff, I just let go! I need ALL my energy to be happy so I'm certainly not going to waste it on negative rubbish OR negative people! Let the bad stuff go and be happy. Try it, what have you actually got to lose?! P.S. It rubs off on other people too!!

Andrew Stunell MP

Andrew Stunell is the Liberal Democrat Member of Parliament for Hazel Grove, Stockport. He is a former Baptist lay preacher.

> " The meaning of life: it's the best chance you ever get to make the world a better place.
>
> The best advice: You can't always do what you like, but you can always like what you do. "

A few facts on life.

You are 3 times more likely to be killed by a flying champagne cork than you are to be killed by the bite of a venomous spider.

Left handed people live slightly shorter lives than right handed people.

Apples, not caffeine, are more efficient at waking you up in the morning.

An average woman consumes approximately 20kg of lipstick in her life.

An octopus has 3 hearts.

Venus is the only planet in the solar system to spin backwards (clockwise).

The elephant is the only mammal that can't jump!

Your body is creating and killing 15 million red blood cells per second.

Months that begin on a Sunday will always have a "Friday the 13th."

Chickens cannot swallow while they are upside down.

Women's hearts beat faster than men's.

A crocodile cannot stick its tongue out.

A few facts on life.

You will weigh less if you weigh yourself when the moon is full.

The average person falls asleep in seven minutes.

For every person on earth there is over 200 million insects.

A rule of three: you can live 3 seconds without blood, 3 minutes without oxygen, 3 days without water and 3 weeks without food.

The average person is about a quarter of an inch taller at night.

Your stomach has to produce a new layer of mucus every two weeks otherwise it will digest itself.

One gallon of used motor oil can ruin about one million gallons of fresh water.

An ant can lift 50 times its own weight and is also able to pull over 30 times its own weight.

The average bed is home to over 6 billion dust mites.

The size of babies' eyes stays the same size from birth, but nose and ears never stop growing.

The greatest recorded number of children one mother had was 69 children.

A 'jiffy' is an actual unit of time for 1/100th of a second.

Fern Britton

The accomplished television presenter Fern Britton is best known for co-presenting the ITV show This Morning. She has written a number of cookery books, as well as her memoirs.

> " Take all competition out of your life. Be confident that you are good enough and have no need to prove it to others . "

Dennis Taylor

Retired snooker player and BBC commentator Dennis Taylor is best known for his over sized glasses and sense of humor. He reached number two in the world rankings and has been a contestant on Strictly Come Dancing.

" When I was growing up as a boy in Northern Ireland, my mother and father always told me to be nice to people and they will be nice to you. I would like to think it worked for me. "

Barbara Clark

Barbara Clark is a best selling author who wrote the book 'The Fight of my Life' after she took the UK Government to court to allow her to be prescribed a life-saving drug.

> " Treat your time on earth like good wine...
>
> Never waste a drop.
>
> Make the most of every moment though sometimes you'd like to stop.
>
> Surround yourself with good thoughts, good people, love and care.
>
> With these few words inside your head,
>
> Trust me you're halfway there. "

Michelle Mone

Michelle is an extremely accomplished entrepreneur and marketer. In November 1996 Michelle set up MJM International Ltd and went on to develop the hugely successful Ultimo bra range.

> " When I was growing up someone close to me used to say "never give up". That has stayed with me my entire life and has helped me through really trying times, particularly when I had a young family and was working day and night to launch my business. Perseverance, in every walk of life is an important lesson. I never thought Ultimo would become the UK's leading lingerie brand and it's all because I never gave up! "

Photo by Gareth Cattermole/Getty Images

Justin Mundy

Justin Mundy, Senior Adviser to HRH The Prince of Wales has 25 years of experience of working on climate change, environment and energy issues and has done so within the public, multilateral and private sectors.

> "Taking a holistic and joined up view of the challenges we face is, I believe, an essential competence in our modern world. Our tendency to form an ever more fragmented and specialist view means that we see the issues before us one by one, rather than as a whole. If we fail to properly appreciate the big picture, then the prospects for us to deal with the related challenges of climate change, poverty reduction, food security, economic recovery, biodiversity protection and long-term human wellbeing will be drastically diminished. If we can see the whole challenge, then we will be better able to see the whole solution."

Dame Ellen MacArthur

English sailor Ellen MacArthur is best known for her solo circumnavigation of the globe in 2007. Ellen has announced her retirement from competitive sailing so she can focus on environmental campaigning.

> " The best bit of advice on life came from my Nan. She always taught me that life holds a lot of treasures and to never forget that. "

Photo by Chris Jackson/WireImage

Some final words for the wise

Whilst working on the content for the Handbook Of Life, we asked our research team to summarise the quotes and maxims they found particularly relevant to life in the modern world:

Many would argue that happiness is what it's all about and the importance of "mental" peace and well being. So understand what brings you, and those around you, happiness and mental peace.

✣

The more we care for the happiness of others, the greater our own sense of well-being becomes.

✣

Invest a few minutes each day thinking about the things that make you happy. These few minutes will give you the opportunity to focus on the positive things in your life and will lead you to continued happiness.

✣

Sometimes you have to plan to achieve the things that make you happy; so don't sit around waiting for divine intervention - make it happen!

✣

…. and, it's never too late to start.

✣

Whilst there are those people who naturally exude energy and happiness there are also those who have a negative outlook and drain other people's happiness and enthusiasm. Better to surround yourself with the former.

✣

There are times that require you to be serious but, when it is appropriate, find a way to make light of a situation that would otherwise make you unhappy.

✤

Happiness and laughter are infectious.

✤

Things will always go wrong – it happens, so be ready for it. You learn most through adversity and strife – recognize this and benefit from it.

✤

Fear is a normal human condition. The brave man is not he who does not feel afraid, but he who conquers his fear.

✤

Talking is easy but listening is a harder and, arguably, a more important skill.

✤

Be confident and true to yourself and what you believe.

✤

Finally, treat your time on earth like good wine...
Never waste a drop.

✤

Which brings us to the last quote in the Handbook......

Professor Ian Morison

Gresham Professor of Astronomy, Prof Ian Morison is based at Jodrell Bank observatory and teaches at the University of Manchester. He lectures widely on astronomy and has contributed to TV and radio programmes.

> The Greeks thought that the Earth was at the centre of the universe and thus we humans were quite important beings. In the last century, as the scale of the universe became apparent and we discovered that our Sun was one of myriads of stars in our Milky Way galaxy, the idea of mediocracy arose. Planets like ours were likely to be very common and so life like ours would be common - we were nothing special.
>
> But more recently, as we have learned more about other solar systems, the view of many astronomers has changed. It took 3.5 thousand million years for simple life to evolve into our human race and it now seems very unlikely that many planets will be able to keep a relatively stable temperature for such a long time - our large Moon may well have played a major role in that. Thus we now suspect that advanced life-forms like ours could be very rare, and it is as likely as not that we are the only advanced civilisation at present existing in our galaxy.
>
> Perhaps our human race **is** special, as is our home, the Earth. Let us hope that we can learn to look after both our planet and ourselves.

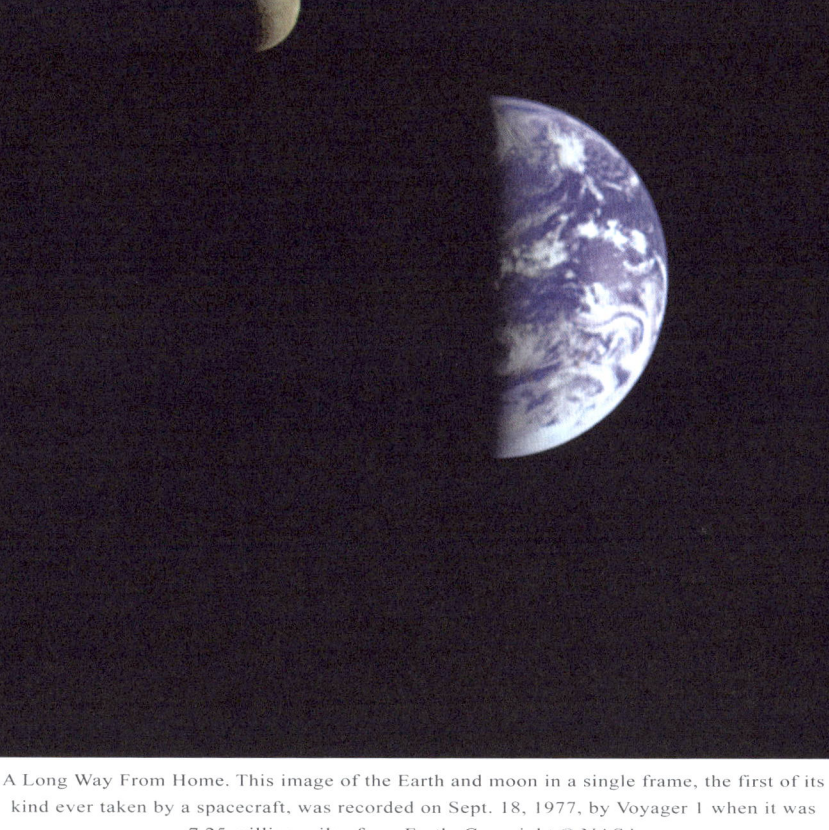

A Long Way From Home. This image of the Earth and moon in a single frame, the first of its kind ever taken by a spacecraft, was recorded on Sept. 18, 1977, by Voyager 1 when it was 7.25 million miles from Earth. Copyright © NASA